MW01264215

SALE

ELIZABETH DOLE

A Leader in Washington

EILEEN LUCAS

The Millbrook Press
Brookfield, Connecticut
A Gateway Biography

Photographs courtesy of: © Michelle Patterson/Gamma Liaison: cover;
Sygma: pp. 6, 11, 20, 29, 42; Duke University Archives: p. 9; AP/Wide World
Photos: pp. 16, 27, 34, 37, 39; © David Hume Kennerly: p. 19; J. P. Laffont/
Sygma: pp. 22; Ira Wyman/Sygma: p. 31, 44; Agence France Press/Corbis-
Bettmann: p. 41.

Library of Congress Cataloging-in-Publication Data
Lucas, Eileen.
Elizabeth Dole : a leader in Washington / Eileen Lucas.
p.   cm. — (Gateway biography)
Includes index.
ISBN 0-7613-0203-4 (lib. bdg.)
1. Dole, Elizabeth Hanford. 2. Women cabinet officers—United States—
Biography. 3. Cabinet officers—United States—Biography.
I. Title. II. Series
E840.8.D63L83   1997
973.92'092—dc21
[B]   97-6270 CIP

Published by The Millbrook Press, Inc.
2 Old New Milford Road, Brookfield, Connecticut 06804

ELIZABETH
DOLE

John and Mary Hanford were trying to decide what to name their newborn baby girl. They already had a son, thirteen-year-old Johnny, named for his father. Now John Hanford thought the baby girl should be named Mary, for her mother. Mary wanted to name the baby Elizabeth Alexander, Mary's grandmother's name. They settled on Mary Elizabeth Alexander Hanford. The little girl would have her own ideas about this. By the time she was two, she'd given herself the nickname Liddy. When she outgrew that, she would use the name Elizabeth.

Liddy had a happy childhood in Salisbury, North Carolina, where she was born on July 29, 1936. It was a friendly town where most people knew one another. Her father owned a flower shop, and her mother volunteered for many church and community activities. The family lived in a big house with a spiral staircase between the first and

Liddy Hanford spent a happy childhood in Salisbury, North Carolina. Although she isn't wearing them in this picture taken when she was four years old, she had already begun wearing glasses.

second floors. Her mother's parents, Mom and Pop Cathey, lived just two houses away. Mom Cathey loved to read the Bible. Little Liddy loved to eat cookies and drink lemonade at her grandmother's house while listening to Bible stories.

Liddy didn't like the glasses she had to wear from the time she was three years old, but she put up with it. When she got older, she would be glad to switch to contact lenses. She had plenty of friends and activities to keep her busy, including piano lessons, summer camps, and pets to care for. She organized a bird club in the third grade and was elected its president. In the sixth grade she started a junior book club and named herself president. She liked to organize things—and to be in charge.

In high school, Liddy was involved in student government. She ran for school president in her senior year. She didn't win, probably in part because in those days this was considered a "boy's job." She was disappointed, but there were still drama club and other activities. Liddy liked to go to parties and have fun, too. Still, she found time to study hard and get good grades. Already she showed the characteristic of always doing her best. Her classmates voted her "most likely to succeed." Many would later remember joking that someday she just might be the First Lady, or the first lady *president*.

After high school Elizabeth decided to attend Duke University because that's where her brother, John, had gone. Her activities in high school had shown her that she enjoyed working with people and was interested in government. She took classes in political science and got involved in student government. In March 1957, she was elected student government president. She also studied hard, was named to the National Honors Society, and was awarded recognition as Leader of the Year at Duke in 1958. In a school newspaper editorial, a fellow student noted, "Through Miss Hanford's direction and imagination the entire University . . . has been left with many long-term improvements."

After graduation Elizabeth had many choices about what to do next. John was now running the family's flower business and offered her a job there. Elizabeth thought about it. She had a boyfriend, and many of her friends were getting married; also, her family would have been pleased to have her settle down to live and work in Salisbury. But Elizabeth decided she wasn't ready for marriage and wanted to see more of the world. She went to work as a secretary in the Harvard Law School Library in Cambridge, Massachusetts. Then she spent a summer in

Elizabeth was a good student and popular with her college classmates at Duke University. In 1958, she was elected May Queen in recognition of her many accomplishments and service to the school.

England at Oxford University, studying English history and government.

Liddy loved to travel and, while in England, decided to visit the Soviet Union. This was during a time when that country was considered by many to be an enemy of the United States. Liddy knew her parents would be worried about this choice, so she wrote down all the reasons she wanted to go there before making an overseas phone call home. She was so well prepared with her reasons that she convinced her parents that she should go. She found the visit interesting and enjoyable.

Elizabeth then went back to school in the United States to study education and government at Harvard. She student-taught in a high school history class and enjoyed it. She didn't want to teach about the government, though; she wanted to be a part of it. In the summer of 1960 she worked as a secretary in the Washington, D.C., office of a senator from North Carolina. She was thrilled to be working in the nation's capital, where all the things she'd been learning about in her classes on government were actually happening. There were two women in the Senate at the time, and Elizabeth went to one of them, Margaret Chase Smith of Maine, for advice. Mrs. Smith told Elizabeth that if she wanted a job in government, she should get a degree in law.

Elizabeth is easy to pick out in this photo taken while she was at Harvard Law School. She was just one of 24 women in a class of 550.

So Elizabeth went back to school again. This time she entered Harvard Law School. She was one of only 24 women in a class of 550. Everyone knew that the work at Harvard Law School was difficult. During exams Elizabeth, like other students, studied for fifteen hours at a time. Somehow, she still managed to have time for friends, too. She was elected president of the international law club and secretary of her class.

In 1965 she graduated from law school and moved back to Washington. There, she passed the bar exam, which meant that she could practice law if she wanted to. Not feeling quite ready for that, she landed a job in the government with the Department of Health, Education and Welfare. Her job was to help plan a conference on the educational problems of deaf people. People said that she did the job well. After the conference, however, the job was over, so Elizabeth started visiting night court to watch and learn more about law.

One night, while she was watching a court session, the judge asked her, "Who are you?"

"I'm Elizabeth Hanford," she replied.

When the judge asked if she was a member of the bar, she said yes, she was. The judge then said, "I have a case for you."

Elizabeth tried to tell him that she wasn't ready, she was just watching. The judge insisted, however. "If you're a member of the D.C. bar, Miss Hanford, you are ready. Come up here."

Elizabeth did as she was told and found herself defending a Greek man who was charged with annoying a lion at the zoo. Elizabeth argued that it was hard to know if the lion was really annoyed since he wasn't there in the courtroom to testify! Then she told the judge that her client promised never to return to that zoo, and he was let go. Elizabeth had won her very first case. For the next year she defended people who had gotten in trouble with the law but had no money for legal advice. She learned a lot about a different side of Washington, and life in general, that way.

In April 1968, Elizabeth began working in an office at the White House. She would be dealing with consumer issues. Consumers are people who buy things. Elizabeth was among those who thought that consumers needed to be protected from certain businesses that were not completely honest about their products. People who worked in this way were called consumer advocates. They tried to help people who had problems with things they bought. They also tried to get companies to give buyers as much information about their products as possible so that people could make wise buying choices. Elizabeth's job was to help get laws passed that would do these things.

The United States government is divided into three branches: the Executive, the Legislative, and the Judicial. The Executive branch includes the president and the people who work for him. The Legislative branch is made up of people who make laws—members of the Senate and House of Representatives. The Judicial branch is made up of the judges and other people who run the court system.

Elizabeth worked in the Executive branch. That meant that a lot of the work to be done, and who would do it, depended on who was serving as president at the time, and what political party that person belonged to. When Elizabeth first went to work in the White House in the mid-1960s, Lyndon Johnson, a Democrat, was president. Elizabeth was a Democrat, too.

In January 1969, Richard Nixon, a Republican, became president. He made some changes in the office Elizabeth worked in. He also brought in a new boss. Elizabeth wondered if the new boss, Virginia Knauer, would like her. Indeed, Mrs. Knauer found Elizabeth to be "a tremendously dedicated worker." She trusted Elizabeth to give speeches that she didn't have time to give herself. Elizabeth became very good at making speeches, as long as she had time to prepare well. She also liked to take her time in making decisions, checking facts to avoid mistakes. Sometimes this slowed things down, but that's the only way Elizabeth knew how to work. One way to make up for this was to work long hours.

One of the things Mrs. Knauer and Elizabeth did together was meet with a senator from Kansas named Bob Dole. It was in the spring of 1972. Senator Dole was chairman of the Republican party's National Committee. Elizabeth and Mrs. Knauer went to talk to him about the party's stand on consumer issues. As they talked, Elizabeth thought that Senator Dole was very good looking.

But there were other men in her life at the time. One of them invited her to attend a Washington Redskins football game with him one weekend. Elizabeth replied that she had too much work to do. Her friend was so excited about his fifty-yard-line seats, however, that he finally talked her into meeting him there. He was not so happy when she showed up with a briefcase full of papers to read during the game. Elizabeth figured she could sit in the sun and read while her friend watched the game! She later admitted that she probably wasn't a very good date that day.

During the next year, Senator Dole began calling Elizabeth. Then one evening he invited her out to dinner. Though he was thirteen years older, they found that they shared many interests and enjoyed talking to each other. Elizabeth learned that Bob Dole had grown up in the small town of Russell, Kansas, during the difficult economic times known as the Depression. During World War II, he enlisted in the army and was sent to Italy. In April 1945, he was severely wounded by shrapnel that tore into his right shoulder. For a while he was almost completely paralyzed, and it was uncertain whether he would live. Slowly he recovered, but he would never be able to use his right arm again.

Bob Dole from Russell, Kansas, served in World War II and was severely injured. When Elizabeth met him, he was a senator and the chairman of the Republican party's National Committee.

Elizabeth also learned that Senator Dole had been married and was now divorced. He had a daughter named Robin, who was a young lady. He had served in the Kansas state legislature and U.S. House of Representatives before being elected senator. Though they were both very busy, Bob and Elizabeth started finding time to be together.

In 1973, President Nixon appointed Elizabeth to the Federal Trade Commission (FTC). She would be one of five commissioners who would make decisions for the government on such matters as commercials on children's television programs, houses that were poorly built, and opportunities for women to get loans or credit. Her selection for this job had to be approved, or accepted, by the Senate. By this time Elizabeth had switched from Democrat to Independent, but some senators wondered how independent she was from the president's Republican policies. FTC commissioners were not supposed to favor one party or another. She was told they would accept her appointment only if consumer advocates supported her. She worked hard to get that support. She visited consumer organizations and stated her views. She testified before a Senate committee, answering questions about her previous job. In the end, the committee was convinced that she would do a good job, and her appointment was approved.

On one of her last days of her old job, Elizabeth was to give a speech in New Jersey. On the way there, a drunk driver hit the rear of the car in which Elizabeth was riding. Her back was hurt, but she went on and gave the speech anyway. Later, however, she went to the hospital and had to stay there for a month. The chairman of the FTC wanted her to start work anyway. He came to her hospital room to give her the oath of office. While sitting in her hospital bed, Elizabeth raised her hand and promised to do a good job. She spent the rest of the time in the hospital reading important papers for her new job.

Elizabeth enjoyed her work as an FTC commissioner. She helped protect people from businesses that tried to cheat people out of their money. She also supported women in business. Another interest was protecting the elderly. Her own grandmother had received wonderful care in a nursing home. She dealt with places that did not give such good care. Elizabeth was finding it very satisfying to be a public servant.

Other people were taking notice of Elizabeth's hard work and talents, too. In 1974, *Time* magazine selected her as one of America's two hundred "Faces of the Future."

Meanwhile Elizabeth Hanford and Bob Dole were growing serious about each other. Once, when they were visiting Elizabeth's family in Salisbury, Bob showed Mrs. Hanford his injured arm and shoulder. "I think you ought to see my problem," he said.

"That's not a problem, Bob," she told him. "That's a badge of honor."

While he was in Kansas campaigning for reelection in 1974, Bob often called Elizabeth long distance to talk at the end of a long day. Soon they were planning a wedding. They were married on December 6, 1975, in the Bethlehem Chapel of the Cathedral of St. Peter and St. Paul in Washington (also known as the Washington National Cathedral). Just before the ceremony, Elizabeth

Her work on consumer affairs made Elizabeth a good candidate for the Federal Trade Commission. After President Nixon appointed her, she had to work hard to gain approval for the job from the Senate.

(19)

Elizabeth Hanford married Senator Robert Dole on December 6, 1975, in Washington, D.C. Both very active in politics and government, they were two busy people who often had to make time to be together.

practiced the wedding vows. As always, she wanted to be well prepared!

After their marriage, Elizabeth and Bob shared his old apartment in the large complex of buildings in Washington known as the Watergate. They watched with interest as Republican President Gerald Ford worked to win the Republican party's nomination in the 1976 presidential race. They wondered whom he would pick to be his vice-presidential running mate. They knew that there was a possibility it would be Bob, but the president was also considering other people. As they checked into a hotel for the Republican convention in Kansas City, Missouri, Elizabeth looked forward to the vacation she and Bob planned to take afterward. But one morning during the convention the president called their room to ask Senator Dole to be his running mate. "Certainly, Mr. President," he responded without hesitation.

Secret Service agents were assigned to protect the Doles. They were given the code names "Ramrod" and "Rainbow." Less than a year after her marriage, Elizabeth found herself the wife of a man running for the vice presidency of the United States. There would be no time for a vacation now. There were rallies and dinners to attend.

When the convention ended, the Ford-Dole campaign began in Bob Dole's hometown of Russell, Kansas. For Elizabeth, it was a very proud moment when she saw

Bob Dole was the vice-presidential running mate of Republican candidate Gerald Ford in the 1976 election. Elizabeth took a leave of absence from her job at the FTC to help with the campaign. Here the Doles are pictured with President Ford and his wife, Betty.

the crowd of ten thousand people who had gathered to cheer for her husband and the president. "I am proof that a person can come from a small town and doesn't need wealth and material things to move ahead," Bob Dole said with tears in his eyes.

There were questions about conflicts between her job as FTC commissioner and her role as a candidate's wife. Should she keep working, or should she resign? Elizabeth decided on a compromise. She took a leave of absence, or extended time off, from her job. This way she could work for the campaign without actually having to quit. Sometimes she stood next to her husband and smiled and waved for the cameras. Other times she gave a speech in one place while Bob spoke in another. In Alabama she fed peanuts to an elephant. In Illinois she played with a kazoo band. She found being part of a national campaign like riding a tiger—"You hold on for dear life," she said, "or else you get devoured." She found campaigning a challenge because things so often came up at the last minute, while she preferred things to be well planned.

As the election drew nearer, she watched Bob in a television debate with the Democratic nominee for vice president, Walter Mondale. Afterward she advised him that the humor he was famous for sometimes hurt him as well as his targets. On election night the Doles sat with Gerald and Betty Ford in the White House watching election results on TV until it became clear that the Democrats had won and Jimmy Carter would become president. Then they went home and soon were back at work, Bob in the Senate and Elizabeth at the FTC.

Since Elizabeth worked in the Executive branch of government, and Bob worked in the Legislative branch, they sometimes found themselves on opposite sides of an issue. Once Bob was one of a group of senators who voted to overturn a decision that Elizabeth had made as an FTC commissioner. The couple later appeared on the TV program *Good Morning, America* to discuss their differing views on another issue. Many people found it interesting to see two intelligent people, who just happened to be married to each other, have a spirited debate. Others wondered if their differences about certain government policies meant that their marriage was in trouble. It wasn't. They loved each other very much and accepted the fact that they sometimes had different opinions about things. One of the main ways they dealt with this was learning to talk very little about their jobs at home. Their time alone together was precious, and they used it to relax. Sometimes they watched movies on TV or used the exercise equipment they bought. Other times they went to plays or concerts.

As the 1980 presidential campaign opened, Bob decided to run for the Republican nomination for president. Other Republicans were interested as well, especially the former governor of California, Ronald Reagan. Elizabeth decided to resign from her job to work in Bob's campaign. Her boss was sorry to lose her, saying that the American consumer owed her "a deep debt of gratitude for a job well done." But by spring Ronald Reagan was winning the primaries, the preelection contests that political parties have in some states, so Bob Dole withdrew from the presidential race to run for reelection as senator. He won that race once again, and became chairman of the Finance Committee, an important job because it dealt with how money would be spent.

Ronald Reagan was elected president, and he appointed Elizabeth to head the White House office of Public Liaison. Her job was to bring together various people and organizations to meet with the president. She called herself "part cheerleader" for the president's policies and "part listening post" for the needs of people. She was described as cheerful and optimistic in doing her work. People noticed that she was good at handling details, and that she had a strong drive for perfection. She often left for work by 7 A.M. and returned home twelve hours later. Bob's schedule was about the same.

One of the results of this intense work schedule was what Elizabeth called "spiritual starvation." She had left little time in her life for God. She found help for this at the Methodist Church she attended. She returned to making Sunday a day of worship and rest. She remembered what her grandmother had taught her—that what we do on our own matters little, what counts is what God chooses to do through us.

In January 1983, President Reagan offered Elizabeth a new job. He asked her to be secretary of transportation. This was sure to be her most challenging job yet. The Department of Transportation (DOT) directs the spending of large sums of money on highways, and is concerned with the transportation of hazardous materials on those highways. It inspects commercial and private aircraft. It is concerned with just about anything that moves and with the people that make things get from one place to another. It is a large agency that deals with a wide variety of complex issues. When considering whether to take the job, Elizabeth decided that "there's something challenging and appealing about going into a situation that's not the easiest and making it work."

Once again Elizabeth appeared before a Senate committee and answered their questions. They must have liked what they heard, for the Senate confirmed her appointment by a vote of 97 to 0. On February 7, 1983, Elizabeth was sworn in by Sandra Day O'Connor, the first woman Supreme Court justice. Elizabeth's mother was there to hold the Bible on which Elizabeth placed her hand in taking the oath of office. Since the U.S. Coast Guard was part of the DOT, Elizabeth became the first woman to head a branch of the armed services.

In her job as the secretary of transportation, Elizabeth's main focus was on safety. Here she inspects a ship in Tampa, Florida, during a trip she made to announce a new motor-vehicle safety program.

The key word for Elizabeth with the DOT was safety. She studied research that indicated that lights in the rear window of a car that lit when the brakes were applied helped to prevent accidents. She saw to it that these lights, nick-named "Dole lights," would be required on cars built in 1986 and after. She was also in favor of both air bags and safety belts in cars. In 1984 none of the states had laws requiring the use of seat belts. By 1990 almost half did, and that number continued to grow. Elizabeth also helped to get the drinking age in many states raised to twenty-one to help reduce the number of young people involved in drunk-driving accidents. She would call her achievements in auto safety "the matter that I'm prouder of than any-thing else in my twenty-five years of government." Some people called her "the Safety Secretary."

As the 1984 campaign approached, there were ru-mors concerning which of the Doles would be running for president or vice president, or both. At a speech in Wash-ington, Bob said that "Dole would not be a candidate in 1984." Elizabeth jumped up and said, "Speak for yourself, sweetheart." Everyone laughed. It turned out that neither Bob nor Elizabeth ran for president or vice president, as President Reagan and Vice President George Bush sought reelection. At the Republican convention, people were seen wearing buttons that said Dole-Dole '88. During the convention, Bob introduced Elizabeth as a speaker. In her speech she talked about the day when a woman would be nominated for president because she was the best candidate, not just because it was time to nominate a woman.

Elizabeth was very busy during the Reagan-Bush campaign. She attended fund-raising dinners and gave speeches all across the country. Not only did Reagan and Bush win in the November election, but the Republicans became a majority in the Senate. That meant that Republican senators could choose the majority leader. They selected Bob Dole. This was a great honor, and to celebrate, Elizabeth gave Bob a miniature schnauzer named Leader. She had found him at a local Humane Society shelter. Both Doles grew to love Leader very much, and took turns taking him for walks and bringing him to their offices.

To celebrate her husband's selection as senate majority leader in 1984, Elizabeth gave Bob a dog, a miniature schnauzer named Leader. Here Elizabeth poses with Leader and another puppy.

During the summer of 1985 the Doles went to China together. They both had their own work to accomplish for the U.S. government, but they enjoyed the opportunity to be traveling together because they often had to travel separately.

Meanwhile, at the DOT, Elizabeth continued to push for safety. She was in favor of random drug testing—giving unexpected tests for drugs to people who worked in transportation, like air traffic controllers and train engineers. Some people didn't like the idea because they said it invaded their privacy. But Elizabeth declared, "No matter how many people oppose me on this, when people are directing traffic in the air and literally hundreds of people could be killed if their judgment is off, no one can tell me it isn't right to test."

Bob again decided to be a candidate for president in the 1988 election. Elizabeth tried to do two jobs: run the DOT and campaign for her husband. She had served as secretary of transportation for four and a half years, longer than anyone else. She enjoyed the challenge that the job presented. But could she continue to divide her time between her job and her husband's campaign? She always expected the best from herself, and it would be difficult to do her best at both of these demanding jobs.

The Doles participate in a Fourth of July parade in New Hampshire during the 1988 presidential campaign. George Bush would win the Republican nomination, and then the election.

On a Sunday afternoon in August 1987, she sat on a bench near the entrance to the Bethlehem Chapel in Washington, where she and Bob had been married. There she decided that she would resign from the DOT. People asked why she should have to quit her job just because her husband was running for president. She answered that she made her decision not because she had to but because she wanted to. In a letter to President Reagan she wrote: "I learned long ago that public life is full of private choices. I have chosen to devote all my time and energies to my husband's campaign for the presidency, not only because Bob needs me, but because I believe the American people need Bob."

After she resigned, Elizabeth worked with Bob on a book they wrote together called *The Doles, Unlimited Partners*. With all she was able to contribute to the campaign, *U.S. News & World Report* magazine called Elizabeth, "her husband's biggest asset." But by spring Vice President George Bush was in the lead in the race for the Republican nomination. Once again, Bob withdrew from the race. Some people wondered if Bush would ask Bob to be his running mate. Later in the campaign, a newspaper writer suggested that Bush should ask Elizabeth to be his running mate. But Bush chose Senator Dan Quayle of Indiana, and together they won the election in November.

In December 1988, President-elect Bush asked Elizabeth Dole to accept the position of secretary of labor. As she considered this important assignment, a number of issues caught her attention. One was unemployment among minorities, especially young people. Another was equal opportunities for women, and still another was her old favorite—safety. These were things she could get excited about. These were worthwhile missions. She accepted, and once again her appointment was easily confirmed.

She jumped into the battle over raising the minimum wage for workers in low-paying jobs. Then she became involved in ending a coal miners' strike. She met with the head of the workers and the head of the company. She got them to agree to let her appoint a mediator. For weeks the mediation went on until a settlement was announced on New Year's Day 1990, and the strike ended. Elizabeth's efforts were praised in many newspapers around the country.

When Communist rule came to an end in Poland, she traveled there to find ways that America and Poland could work together. She was reminded of how satisfying it was to work on things that really helped people. She was thinking about this when she received a call from the American Red Cross (ARC) early in 1990. They told her that they were looking for a new leader with qualifications just like hers. Would she be interested in being president of the American Red Cross?

The American Red Cross is a large organization. It provides help to victims of disasters such as hurricanes, tornadoes, and floods. It also collects and distributes more than half the blood that is used in hospitals around the country. Most of its workers are volunteers.

Elizabeth was interested, but the timing was wrong. There was still so much work to be done at the Department of Labor (DOL). As she continued that work, she encouraged students to work hard in school so that they could get good jobs afterward. She promoted new kinds of programs to train people for jobs in the 1990s and beyond.

Her work with the Department of Labor sometimes took Elizabeth to schools, where she encouraged students to work hard. Here she watches two children in a Miami school solve a math problem.

In a 1990 poll, *McCall's* magazine readers picked Elizabeth as their choice for the first woman president. While Elizabeth refused to indicate whether she would ever run for that office, she did say, "I am convinced that in my lifetime a woman will break through the political glass ceiling and be elected president."

Meanwhile, the American Red Cross called Elizabeth again. They still thought she would be the perfect leader for them, but they were going to have to pick someone soon. It was a now-or-never opportunity. Elizabeth knew that her greatest satisfactions came from helping people. It seemed that with the Red Cross she'd be able to dedicate herself to that kind of work. She decided to take the job.

At the end of October 1990, Elizabeth announced that she would be leaving the Department of Labor. She explained her reasons for leaving: "I will join an army that includes more than a million volunteers in this country, more than 250 million around the world—those whose sole mission is to meet human needs, to improve the quality of human life."

After taking a few months to learn about the new job, Elizabeth officially began work at the American Red

Cross in February 1991. To show her support for Red Cross volunteers, she decided not to accept her salary for her first year so that she, too, would be a volunteer. Over the next five years she would donate about a half million dollars in speaking fees to the Red Cross.

When Elizabeth joined the ARC, it was going through some difficult times. Funds were low after a number of hurricane and earthquake relief efforts. Most serious, there was concern over the safety of the nation's blood supply. Because of the AIDS epidemic, people were worried about the chances of getting AIDS while giving blood or from receiving blood that had come from someone with AIDS.

After meeting with a number of people at the Red Cross, Elizabeth announced a series of major changes in the way that blood would be collected and handled. She would spend a great deal of money to bring the training and equipment involved in this process up-to-date. It was called "the most ambitious and far-reaching project the Red Cross had ever undertaken."

Over the next several years, Elizabeth's work would take her to many places. She went to Saudi Arabia and Kuwait after the Persian Gulf War. She visited relief operations in Rwanda, in Africa, and called it "the hardest expe-

In 1992, Elizabeth visited Florida as president of the American Red Cross to help victims of Hurricane Andrew. A year later, she returned to help prepare and educate residents in the event of other hurricanes.

rience of my life." Many people were killed in a terrible civil war there, and many others were driven from their homes by the fighting. She went to Florida in 1992 after Hurricane Andrew struck, and to Hawaii when it was devastated by Hurricane Iniki.

Then in April 1995, Bob Dole announced again that he would seek his party's nomination for president. Once again Elizabeth had a difficult decision to make about her career. In October 1995 she decided to take a temporary leave from her duties at the Red Cross to campaign for her husband. She said that if Bob was elected, she would continue with her job at the Red Cross, as well as fulfill her responsibilities as First Lady. Since the national headquarters for the Red Cross is only a block away from the White House, she even thought she would be able to make it home for lunch!

This time Bob Dole did well in many of the pre-election primaries. By the end of March, it became clear that he would finally be the Republican party's nominee. It appeared that it would be difficult, however, for him to defeat the Democratic candidate, President Bill Clinton, who was running for reelection. To show how determined he was to win the election, Bob announced in May 1996 that he would resign from the Senate after twenty-seven years of service to devote himself to the campaign. It was an announcement that left Dole and a number of colleagues in tears.

During the following months both Doles campaigned long and hard. Often this meant that they were apart for

During the presidential campaign of 1996, Elizabeth and Bob Dole signed copies of their book, **The Doles: Unlimited Partners,** *at a New York bookstore.*

long periods of time. To make up for this, they would check in with each other's staff. "Make sure you fit in some time for Bob to rest," Elizabeth requested of her husband's schedulers. "Did you give Elizabeth time to eat?" he asked her people.

At the Republican party's convention in San Diego, California, on August 14, Elizabeth Dole gave a speech in which she said of her husband: "He wants to make a difference, a positive difference, for others because he cares, because that's who he is." But on November 5, 1996, the American people chose Bill Clinton. Once again the Doles faced defeat and had decisions to make about the future.

For Elizabeth, that meant returning to work at the American Red Cross. In April 1997, she visited people whose homes had been damaged by floodwaters in Grand Forks, North Dakota. The day before, President Clinton had told people that the government would help them. Elizabeth Dole said that the Red Cross would help them, too. "When people go through a situation like this, it's good to have some help," she said.

Throughout her career, Elizabeth has talked about creating more opportunities for women. She believes that women should be able to make choices about their future that are right for themselves and their families.

"Today," she says of American women, "we wear the robes of a judge, the face mask of a surgeon, the pinstripes of a banker. We teach on campuses, peer through microscopes, design buildings, and run businesses. Some

Bob Dole came closer to being president in 1996 than he had in any of the other campaigns in which he participated. At the Republican national convention in August, the Doles waved to supporters.

Elizabeth Dole has demonstrated her caring for people and her leadership skills in every role she has taken on. She is pictured here during a 1996 Red Cross mission, visiting with children in the African nation of Somalia.

of us write the laws that other women enforce. Some build rockets for others to ride into space. The most energetic of all run a home and raise a family. No role is superior to another."

A long time has passed since she was elected president of the third-grade bird club. She is now "President Dole" at the American Red Cross. Could she be president of the United States someday? That remains to be seen. But one way or another, Elizabeth Hanford Dole is likely to continue to be a leader and to serve her country and its people well.

Timeline

July 29, 1936 Mary Elizabeth Alexander Hanford is born in Salisbury, NC.

1954   Graduates from high school in Salisbury, NC.

1958   Graduates from Duke University, Durham, NC.

1960   Receives master's degree from Harvard University, Cambridge, MA.

1965   Receives law degree from Harvard University.

1966	Employed in Department of Health, Education and Welfare, preparing conference on education for the deaf.
1967	Practices law in Washington, D.C.
1968	Works in the White House office on consumer affairs issues.
1973	Named to the Federal Trade Commission (FTC).
1975	Marries Senator Bob Dole.
1976	Bob Dole is nominated the Republican candidate for vice president. President Gerald Ford and Dole lose to Jimmy Carter and Walter Mondale.
1980	Elizabeth resigns from the FTC to help Bob seek the Republican nomination for president. Ronald Reagan wins the nomination and the election.
1981	Reagan appoints Elizabeth to the White House office of Public Liaison.
1983	Appointed secretary of transportation.
1987	Resigns to support Bob's campaign for president.
1988	George Bush wins the nomination and the election.
1989	Bush appoints Elizabeth secretary of labor.
1991	Becomes president of the American Red Cross.
1995	Takes leave of absence from the Red Cross to campaign with Bob for presidency.
1996	President Bill Clinton defeats Bob Dole. Elizabeth Dole returns to work at the American Red Cross.

Further Reading

Feinberg, Barbara Silberdick. *The Cabinet*. New York: Twenty-First Century Books, 1995.

Gilbo, Patrick. *The American Red Cross*. New York: Chelsea House, 1987.

Mulford, Carolyn. *Elizabeth Dole: Public Servant*. Hillside, NJ: Enslow Publishers, 1992.

Patrick, Diane. *The Executive Branch*. New York: Franklin Watts, 1994.

Steins, Richard. *Our Elections*. Brookfield, CT: The Millbrook Press, 1994.

Index